Customer Service King

By Joseph Vaudy

How to Go From Average to Excellent

Joseph Vaudy

Intro

How do we go from average to excellent, from being unrecognizable in the crowd to standing out, from starting at the bottom to being at the top in our field? How do we understand the mechanism required to be everything our employer is calling us to be, so we can achieve the status and the benefits of a Customer Service King? How do we move from being a deficit as an employee to being the role model, the most valuable asset that any employer would ask for?

How do we compete in the twenty-first century, where employers are looking for one out of thousands who will take their company to the next level, those who will embody the mission as well as understand the vision of that company?

Every great company knows customer service is vital, and that the business cannot rely simply on the direct service provided. It also relies on those who are in place to serve the customer; initial contact with the customer is critical and that, in itself, will decide whether you will have a loyal customer or not. Therefore, the bottom line of any business is dependent on having an all-star team.

This short book will take you through some of the most important steps to becoming everything your company is looking for and more in the customer service arena. By applying the information in this book, you will become the best you can be while enjoying the prizes and influence that comes with being at the top, otherwise known as Customer Service King.

I've done it; now let me show you how to do it, too.

Table of Contents

Joseph Vaudy

Joseph Vaudy

AMTRAK   November 2013

SOUTHEAST
LONG-DISTANCE SERVICES

Vaudy Joseph, train attendant, with his wife, Alexzandra, and daughter, Al'tayia

Joseph excels
at customer service

For Vaudy Joseph, Miami train attendant, customer service means treating others as oneself. He considers every person he meets to be unique and beautiful.

"It takes a lot to have good customer service," he said. "I'm blessed to have this job."

Joseph tries to be aware of every person's issues through conversation. That way, he can treat the person in perspective. Joseph draws upon his faith to assist his endeavors.

"When I'm challenged, my values keep me in check," he said.

Joseph plans to emphasize gratitude while talking with Miami station new hires about customer service.

"When you're conscious of how lucky you are, you can treat others better," he said.

At home, Joseph is writing a book on true success in life, based on good relationships with God and others. He began the 200-page book this year and plans to finish it by April 13, 2014. He writes two to three hours a week, often putting in ideas he learns at work.

"Other people can tell you a lot of things about how to be truly successful," he said.

Besides his work and his book, Joseph cherishes time with his family, especially his daughter Al'tayia, and participating in church activities.

Haynes enjoys new career

Kendall Haynes, Jacksonville baggage agent, watches and learns. He wants to excel at his job to increase his abilities.

"Once you have a foundation, you can go on from there," said Haynes, who joined Amtrak June 5. "Ensure you learn things first, and the speed will come."

He served four years in the Marines and learned the value of training. The most important aspect, he believes, is to learn everything properly.

"As they say in the Marines, 'You train like you fight; you fight like you train,'" Haynes said.

He enjoys customer service, especially when his growing expertise puts passengers at ease. He likes helping others.

Haynes qualified as a Safe-2Safer observer Oct. 4. He supports enhanced safety practices, such as scanning the work area, suggesting improvements and responding promptly.

"It's good to get somebody else's feedback and have a mindset of being safe," he said.

Haynes continues learning about ticketing, safety, customer service and operating the forklift.

"My job is to be good at what I'm doing now, which will lead to other opportunities," he said.

5

Joseph Vaudy

Silver Service team members participate in the celebration. From left to right: Vaudy Joseph, Jackie Rutledge, Cheryl Smith, David Lambert, Ashok Kumar, Christopher Beyer.

Southeast Region Celebrates Outstanding Employees

In support of our Strategic Plan, various efforts to improve our customers' experience are taking place in the company. On February 21, 2014, the *Silver Service* route group celebrated the efforts of employees from Mechanical, On-Board Service, Stations and Engineering with 120 awards. Among the award categories were perfect attendance, above and beyond, cleanest restrooms and other services that improve the customers' experience. Train Attendant Vaudy Joseph was honored as the "customer service king" for receiving the most praise in the entire country.

The employees were rated by customer reviews, inspections en route by managers and fellow employees, highest revenue aboard the train and chefs who prepared the most meals.

"It is important that we recognize our people on a regular basis and let them know that we appreciate all the work they do," said *Silver Service* Route Director Karen Shannon. "We recognize our top performers in a financially responsible manner and the response has been overwhelming. It is the first time that we included everyone. It is more than those who deal directly with the customers but also the ones behind the scene."

Celebrations also took place on April 10, 2014, for employees of the *Auto Train* and celebrations are coming for the *Crescent* and *City of New Orleans* employees in early May.

Living the Safety and Security Goal

One of our strategic goals is Safety and Security to ensure that every passenger and employee goes home injury-free every day. On March 20, 2014, Amtrak Emergency Management and Corporate Security (EMCS) Regional Manager David B. Albert graduated from the Federal Emergency

Emergency Management and Corporate Security Regional Manager David B. Albert (right) is congratulated by Emergency Management Institute Acting Deputy Superintendent Edward Smith (left) after completing the National Emergency Management Academy training.

6

Joseph Vaudy

The Day I Became King...

It was a day of celebration, gifting, and crowning; I was called to receive the greatest honor of the day, I was crowned the Customer Service King on account of receiving the most praises nationwide, for a billion dollar corporation. I did not know I would be exalted and given the pleasure of sharing the stage with some of the most prominent figures in the company; I knew I was there to be recognized, but to have received so much shocked and humbled me. To understand how I felt, you need to know something about me. I have done many things in my life; I was master of all trades, but an expert at none. I have never been considered the shining star, the go-to guy, the expert, or the role model; however, on that day, I was recognized as nothing less than that. So it is an understatement to say a star was born. Going forward, nothing would ever be the same, and I went on for the next two years, dominating the praise board on a monthly basis, solidifying myself as being worthy of the acknowledgement directed toward me. During those two years, I received hundreds of praises from customers nationwide, fellow employees, as well as supervisors, making it clear that it was no accident or mistake; it was clear my awards were not simply a sign of favoritism, as they were awarded by people who owed me nothing. Looking back, I feel humbled and blessed. I never set out to be number one in my field; it was simply the benefit of a change that was taking place in my personal life, which had spilled into every other aspect of my life, including my professional life.

Truth is, the young man who started with the company at the age of twenty-three, was very different from the recipient of the accolades, awards, and the praises at age twenty-six. Nonetheless, the seed of greatness in the area of customer service and public relations was always there, and had been recognized long before when I was a cashier with a big smile at McDonalds.

However, it wouldn't be fair to only discuss the glitz and glamour; I want to share my shame as well as my joy, my weaknesses as well as my strengths.

At the age of twenty-three, I was given a remarkable opportunity; it was life changing to say the least. I was one of twelve great men and women to be employed by Amtrak, joining a pool of about 25,000 employees from all around the country. For a kid like me born in a third world country, an entry-level salary of about forty to fifty thousand dollars was a blessing I couldn't pass up. I had signed on to work as a train attendant. I travelled back and forth from Miami to New York, spending about fifty hours on the train, meeting people's needs, as well as boarding and detraining folks. I travelled through small towns like Palatka, Kingstree, Hamlet, as well a big cities such as Miami, Tampa, Washington, Philadelphia, New York, and many more.

As a young kid who had not yet developed into a man, I was full of flaws, vices, and self-destructive desires; I had no awareness that I could very well be the cause of my own destruction. Having watched my mother achieve so much because of the same opportunity she had received from Amtrak almost two decades before me, there was no doubt in my mind that this could definitely change my life for the better. If only I could manage to be faithful to it, the way it could be faithful to me. But the truth is, at the time, I couldn't muster such faith. I was caught in a web that was threatening to throw all the potential opportunities away. I had developed bad habits; failing to value my job, put things into perspective or prioritize my life in the way that was necessary.

I had an appetite for women, and being in a position of authority, in an environment that was flooded with some of the most attractive women from all over the world, I was slowly digging a hole for myself that I would need a long rope to pull myself out of. It was about meeting my selfish desires, and seeing just how many women I could charm or win over just to satisfy my ego. All along, knowing in the back of my mind that if anyone were ever to call corporate for my unprofessionalism, I would be in a pool of trouble, possibly losing the one opportunity that was there to change my life. My lust had grown into something that was affecting my relationships outside of Amtrak and killing my performance and potential on the job, because my energy and focus were being spent in the wrong places. Needless to say, my focus was far from customer service, though my talent in that area had enabled me to stay afloat even while I was flirting with termination.

Every time an attractive woman boarded the train, it was another opportunity for me to turn on my charm. Fair to say, many of those women probably felt pressured to entertain my foolishness simply because of my authoritative nature on the train. In such cases, partiality was evident because my focus was never about acknowledging everyone, it was more so about picking the ones I wanted to speak to or help, the ones who I felt were attractive. It didn't help that I was in a toxic environment where many applauded, encouraged, and shared my views, as well as partook in the same actions I had fallen into so deeply.

However, that was just one of many issues that could have caused me to be fired or could have found myself in a pool of trouble. Because, back then, I also had an issue with people not respecting me the way I believed they should. I believed it was up to me to get in their face and demand they treat me with respect. I had no comprehension of submission and the concept of authority. I had no understanding of the fact that I had signed on the dotted line when accepting the job, that I would follow the guidelines as stipulated by Amtrak.

Now I'm assuming you must be asking yourself how a guy like that ended up at the top of the board, received award after award, sat on the service excellence committee and was crowned as the customer service king, and became a force to be reckoned with in the area of customer service? I can't even say it was intentional. I would have to say it was a change in my life which drastically redirected my focus, renewed my mind, and reshaped my perception that allowed me to achieve all I've managed to achieve in so little time. Truthfully, it was an act of grace that changed it all. I suspect for others who have shifted from a life of self-destruction to living a vibrant, energetic, inspiring, and productive life, many things could have influenced the turn. I can only speak for me. The power of grace, a second chance, mercy, and forgiveness in my life was undeniable.

Here was a guy who was swimming in lust; enslaved by selfish desires which could have led him to the unemployment line. He thought violence was the way to obtain respect; he had overdosed on pride and could not submit properly to those in authority. I thought there was no hope for him, but I'm thankful that grace was sufficient to take me over **the bridge** from being lost to being found, from average to excellent, from a defected employee to a great asset, from average to Customer Service King.

What happened along that **bridge** was that I found my identity, value, and purpose. My mind was being renewed; and that man no longer lived. I was a new creation, I had been injected with new blood, I was alive, there was clarity, I was learning what it was to be a man, what it meant to properly submit and the benefits of it, learning to be faithful to not only my now wife and daughters, but also to be faithful to the opportunities of life, to be a great steward of the blessings given to me. Obviously, Amtrak was one of those many blessings; it enabled me to provide for my family in a way most jobs couldn't, but it had also now become an avenue for me to practice self-control, patience, servant-hood, and the art of being long-suffering. I came to understand that with every move, accountability and ownership were necessary, so my bosses were no longer the managers—rather it was the newfound values and morals and the force within that were my ultimate supervisors. They would be present with me in my hotel rooms when I was away from home, away from my wife and family, so the idea of having someone in there with me who wasn't my wife was out of the question. I couldn't be partial anymore. In the same manner that I was loved, I would also have to love. My attention could no longer be directed toward the attractive ladies on the train, but to all—the babies, the teens, the young adults, the grandmas, the poor, the rich, etc. I could not war with everyone simply because they talked to me in a manner I did not like or appreciate. I would have to accept that, when dealing with a large amount of people, forgiveness and mercy was something I'd be willing to give to all, whether they deserved it or not, and I would have to embody grace, the same grace that had changed the course of my life. My new motto would be to "do what I do with a spirit of excellence, investing my heart, mind, and strength into my job, just as I am required." By understanding that my transformation occurred by the grace that was given to me, I could no longer complain of the changes and the small things I did not like; I would learn to focus on the bigger picture, and until I moved on to something different or better, this was the source of what was sustaining my family and me. So I must remain grateful, thankful, and faithful to it, not just for my sake, but also for the sake of those around me. Last, but not least, it was now my duty to let my light shine as a testimony of the goodness that was extended to me and the power of grace and a second chance.

Therefore, as I took on this journey of renewing my mind, I was slowly becoming what I had not intended to become—Customer Service King. With those changes came hundreds of praises and now it's time for me to help others reach that point. My newfound values, morals, principles and clarity had enabled me to reach that point. So I know without a doubt this small book, with its core principles, will add something to your game that will push it up a few notches, something your boss will undoubtedly notice and reward.

Know Thyself

To properly deal with people, I believe there are two big questions employees must be able to answer. The first one is: Who am I? In this regard, you answer three questions: the identity question, the value question, and the purpose question.

The next big question that must be answered is: Truly, where am I going? This deals primarily with short-term and long-term goals.

When answering the identity question, people often go straight to race, profession, gender, religion, etc. Although our identity is constructed by these things, they can change—they are so broad that it does not really say anything about who we are. Some say, "I am a doctor." Well, what happens when you retire? Does it mean you no longer have an identity? Some say, "I am African American." Well, what does that mean or what does it say about you? Next to nothing.

Having a good grip on who you are helps you to put things into perspective. It fosters confidence and helps you to understand your self-worth and value; it also gives you a sense of reason for being, purpose, or so on. It stabilizes your life and helps you to be true to your values and morals. Having nothing to prove gives you a sense of accountability that the buck stops with you; that working is part of your purpose. It gives you a sense that you are going somewhere; it helps you realize that the job you find yourself doing is a bridge to something bigger, that nothing is beneath one who understands that through any journey, there must be sacrifice.

Joseph Vaudy

It is important that one is grounded when working in a profession that involves dealing with people, as dealing with conflicts and disappointments is inevitable. Also, in a culture where arguing with a customer can get you fired, you must always keep a sound mind and a cool head, knowing that no insult defines you. Just because someone makes a comment or has an unfavorable opinion of you, this does not mean you have to respond. When you know who you are, you can stand by your values and morals and not waver or jeopardize your job or livelihood. When you know where you're going, you do what you're doing with a spirit of excellence, knowing it is simply a stepping-stone on your greater path.

As you envision yourself becoming king, be sure you are moving on steady ground. While distractions will come, if you are focused, you will be able to do what you're doing not only with a spirit of excellence, but in a humbling manner and with a spirit of forgiveness for anything that anyone might do or say to you on your journey.

Understanding the Value Formula

What is the value formula? Over the past few years, I've learned to respect this formula for its truthfulness, but also because of the role it has played in my decision making and how I prioritize different aspects of life, whether it's my career, marriage, or my life as a father. I've learned that whether we are conscious of it or not, we place a value on everything in our lives, and it is reflected in our decisions or actions on a daily basis. I've come to see that whatever we don't value properly, we abuse and whatever we abuse, we eventually lose. That formula is truly relevant no matter where we place it in our lives. For example, if I don't properly value my relationship, I begin to abuse that relationship or person until they reach the point of breaking and they decide to walk away from the relationship. The abuse could take the form of being unfaithful, physically abusive, or engaging in emotionally or spiritually destructive behaviors. Sadly, the person doing the cheating, abusing or so on, often does not necessarily want the consequence of their actions, whether it's a divorce or a break up. However, because they failed to assess the true value of that person or relationship, it allows them to make self-destructive decisions. They fail to properly prioritize things in their lives.

Sad to say, I've been on the unhappy end of this spectrum in many aspects of my life prior to my spiritual awakening; I cheated on women, as well as spiritually abused them. I also abused my job. However, the truth is, I had not assessed the proper value of my job or the relationship I was in, but I'm glad to say when I finally understood the value of my job and my marriage, it dramatically opened the door to me striving to be king; for once, my focus on my job was in the proper place, and it was to perform at the level I knew I could.

So ask yourself: Are you placing the wrong value on your job? Have you grown complacent? Are you doing things that clearly jeopardize or compromise your success as an employee? Being king is impossible until you truly prioritize and place the right value on the important things. Sometimes, this requires sitting down to count our blessings rather than focusing on what we are lacking. We need to assess what is important in our lives; what is and what isn't serving us.

When I began to do that, my focus at work became delivering the best customer service possible. I removed pleasure from business, and changed my morals as well as how I valued my relationship, my marriage, my family, and my job.

If you want to be king, ask yourself: What are the great things about my job? How would I feel if I lost those things? What does this job mean to me right now? What does my employer expect of me?

Understanding Submission

The definition of submission is "the action or fact of accepting or yielding to a superior force or to the will or authority of another person (encyclopedia.com)." It is one of the scariest concepts to accept for a lot of people, whether it is a husband or a wife, a human being and his God, son and a father, or an employee and his employer. Perhaps people fear being taken advantage of, losing one's identity, one's will, or the feeling of being less than.

However, I would say the concept is, in a nutshell, a must for society to be successful. First and foremost, when thinking of submission, it usually falls in the line of **submission to a higher power, submission to an employer, and submission to authority, whether it is familial, or civilian and those who protects him or her**, for example, law enforcement.

In the case of **submission to a higher power,** an individual, whether Christian, Muslim, or Jew, takes their identity from that higher power, as well as the ideology that comes with it, forsaking his or her way of viewing things but instead leaning to the authority of that higher power to give structure, wisdom, understanding, and direction.

In the case of **an employer, an employee** is paid to not only perform a set of tasks but also to adopt the mission and vision of the company, whether they fully agree with it or not. Furthermore, the company is structured in a certain way that even if you disagree with some of its practices or ideas, if you desire to obtain a paycheck, you must respectfully subject yourself to its authority in the end. It doesn't mean your idea is wrong, only that the last word is always reserved for the one in authority.

How does this relate to customer service? First, you must understand that your submission to authority is protection, and it is more of a plus than a minus. As long as you move according to the will of the employer, you will continue to be paid. It doesn't mean you are less than your employer is or that your idea doesn't count; there must always be a decision maker, especially in the midst of chaos. Making peace with that structure is vital, otherwise you will become more of a liability than an asset to any company.

Submitting is learning to follow as you lead, understanding the chain of command, fulfilling your duties, and completing your tasks so you will receive the approval of your employer. This doesn't mean you can't pitch your ideas, but in the end, what the person in authority says, goes. If you move according to the bylaws of your company, they have an ethical responsibility to protect you and to continue to provide for you.

Mastering Servant hood

"The greatest among you will be your servant." Mark 9:35

Serving your way to the top

When people think of achieving a certain level of greatness, they most often fail to realize that the primary ingredient necessary for anyone to achieve greatness is actually servanthood. The greatest among us are truly the servants, those who address a need in society, whether it is an idea, a product, or excellent customer service. See, the truth of the matter is, those we consider great— Jesus Christ, Steve Jobs, Henry Ford, Thomas Edison, and Martin Luther King—understood this idea to be true. They understood that they could serve as many people as possible through their idea, service, or product, and that this would lead to achieving the greatness they aspired.

Every business is fighting for one thing: to serve as many people as possible. That is the bottom line at the end of the day and that is why mastering servanthood is critical to any employee striving for greatness in any line of work. Therefore, my success as an employee is dependent on how many people I serve, and how excellent my service is; they are the ones who ultimately crown me as king.

The great thing about being an employee is that my responsibility is simply to sell a product in the best possible way. I don't have to worry about creating the product. It exists, it has been tested, and it is selling already, so my focus is to simply maximize and capitalize on the service. However, doing that effectively requires mastering the qualities of being a great servant.

Qualities of a great servant

One of the greatest qualities of a servant is their mastery of **humility**. This gives them the ability to handle criticism, as well as praise, properly, to learn and incorporate what works while dropping what doesn't, to put their ego or pride to the side, and to understand submission and respect for authority. Being humble means understanding that you don't know it all and that you can always learn more; it also means understanding that the customer comes before your feelings or desires.

Another quality of a great servant is their **integrity**. See, customers love honesty. Though the truth can hurt, a servant who is honest and who shows character and sincerity is one who people will flock to simply because they can trust them to tell the truth. They have credibility.

Great servants are often **motivated by love.** Love for the service they provide, love for the people they provide it to, and most importantly, they love what they stand for.

They often move with **passion**. They are motivated by their passion to serve something they believe in, and serving it in a way that reflects their values.

They are also an **expert**–this means they understand the product or service well and are able to articulate and provide assistance when needed. They are the go-to person whenever there's an issue.

They put **service before selfishness**, and also are **focused on service, not the crown or prize**. They understand that nothing should be taken personal in business, and that pleasure and business should not mix. As a result, they are able to separate their business life from their personal life, pride, and ego. They understand the ultimate goal is to provide excellent service and that everything else will follow suit. This means there's no need to focus on being number one or on the prize; instead, the focus should be on elevating service to the point where you are able to dominate and not compete; this automatically places them in the number one spot as king.

They are **leaders by heart**, simply because they are willing to take the lead when others won't. They are willing to risk failing for the satisfaction of winning, while the average person is handicapped by either fear or complacency.

Last, but not least, **they are able to anticipate needs**, meaning they are visionaries, people who can see what's missing to make the product or service better. This also proves that they understand the customer and the product well.

Although there are many more qualities or characteristics that could be mentioned, these are truly some of the most important qualities in a great servant: **integrity, humility, motivated by love, passion, possess expert knowledge, place service before selfishness, focus on customer service instead of the prize, they are leaders by heart, and lastly, they are able to anticipate needs.** With these qualities in place, servanthood is truly mastered and, before you know it, a king is crowned.

Joseph Vaudy

How to Standout

"I want to be different. If everyone is wearing black, I want to be wearing red." Maria Sharapova

In a world where so many people are average, it takes little effort to really standout. The truth of the matter is most people are content with doing the bare minimum; their potential and creativity is left untapped, making room for those who care to be different, who are not afraid to be the oddball until they begin to shine and standout. See, I love the idea of standing out; I'm passionate about it, the idea of creating magic out of nothing, seeing what is, and daring to manifest what it can be. It is the way of the twenty-first century, where the old ways are becoming obsolete, where creativity is needed, where those who are able to take the initiative are sought, where those who standout will be promoted and the average will be cut, and where employers are looking for leaders. The dream of every recruiter is to find those who notice that everyone is turning left into a ditch, and decide to go right into the future. Standing out is not just an idea, it is a lifestyle, a mindset; once it is adopted, a king is born.

The formula is simple. First, you must **understand what average is**, **understand what is missing**, and simply **fill in the blank**.

How do we understand what average is? Average is what everyone is stuck on: the old tricks, the old ways of doing things. Looking at what people who have been with the company for a while became comfortable doing, a bunch of habits that keep them in bondage to average. What is worse is that new hires begin

22

to reflect the same thinking as those who have been with a company for a longer period. It is the perfect scenario for those who are looking to standout. Once it becomes clear what the average are doing and thinking, then it's time to unleash the creativity within. This moves us into the next step of the formula, **understanding what is missing**. It could be as simple as everyone is always mad and frowning when dealing with the customers, and I decide to be happy and smile; you deliver your food in a plastic bag, but I decide to place it on a tray with a tablecloth and wrapped silverware. How simple were those two examples? Simple as can be! However, to the customer, it is golden. The difference is clear: apples and oranges. What the average employees lack can be a mindset or attitude needed for that particular business, or a set of actions that can elevate the customer service or customer experience to the next level. Once it is noticed, it is easy to move into the last piece of the formula, which is simply to **fill in the blank.** Filling in the blank is what separates the average from the greats in any area of life, including customer service. Why? Because it involves something that average employees are not willing to do. That's application, to study and notice what is average, to figure out what's missing, and to take the initiative to bring the ideas into application. It is out of those actions that a king is born, the refusal to be one in the thousands, but instead choosing to step away from the crowd, and applying what you believe is missing for the betterment of your employer.

Exceeding Expectations

The art of exceeding expectations is seductive at best. It takes hold of the customer and refuses to let go; it leaves them in awe and wanting to come back for more. Over the years, I have seen how important and fruitful this idea can be to anyone who decides to use it. See, the mind works in an amazing way. We are wired with a collection of habits and experiences that we take everywhere we go. Often, it is the last experience we remember, whether it was good or bad. My job as a Customer Service King is to turn the bad into good, and the good into better, if it is possible. It is about anticipating the customer's point of satisfaction, outthinking the customer for their own benefit, and making service a focus; it is also my role to see that my customer service and the experience that I'm selling is being perfected on an ongoing basis. I am never satisfied with my last impression; instead, I attempt to change what doesn't work while perfecting and mastering what does—to give the customer an experience he or she will not forget.

There are four things that will help in regard to exceeding expectations:

Make going above and beyond a habit. Don't be content with just meeting expectations, aim for excellence.

How do we **make going above and beyond** a habit? Remember: human beings are creatures of habit; the things we continually do become so ingrained in us that they become who we are, and that in itself has the power to work for us or against us. This means the good habits will benefit us in the long run, while the bad ones can lead to our self-destruction. For example, you end up with a six-pack and you learn to maintain it out of the habit of exercising regularly. So to be a customer service king, you must adopt the habit of doing what successful people do on a continuing basis until it becomes second nature and a part of who you are. Also, part of that involves making going above and beyond the norm, meaning being self-sacrificial and doing what you are not required to do in order to satisfy the customer and put a smile on their face.

To do that, **you can't be content with just meeting expectations.** Achieving more than we expect will create a lasting impression. I cannot be content with average performance, as it is such a competitive world. I can never become complacent, because average is obsolete; creativity and excellence is slowly becoming the norm.

Also, **you must take customers beyond satisfaction**, which simply means aim for that lasting impression that will keep them coming back and looking for more.

Last, but not least, **give customers a taste of excellence**, meaning leave them drooling, with nothing to say other than to praise the service.

Joseph Vaudy

Winning with People

"People don't care how much you know until they know how much you care." John C. Maxwell

To win with people, I believe you must be intentional enough to have a strategy, but spontaneous enough to be able to put it to the side when necessary. When we think of professions where you must master the art of winning with people, the following come to mind: a salesperson, a politician, a minister, and an entertainer. We watch as the politicians maneuver through the crowd, smiling, shaking hands, and kissing babies. They smile as they acknowledge the crowd and silently say, "I care deeply about your needs, I speak your language, I'm just like you. Without you I can't make it, your vote is important, every vote counts. I am for the common man as well as the business man, the homeless man under the bridge, and the penthouse CEO." It is an art in itself. One would hope such a figure would be humble and possess a great dose of integrity. The truth is winning with people takes a little bit of intent, spontaneity, and a balance of goofiness and seriousness. In addition, one needs to possess the temperament to deal with all types of people, be cool as a cucumber under pressure, and charismatic enough to carry the crowd.

The reality is, no matter what the profession is, we are all selling and serving; therefore, we should be trying to win with people, whether it is the nurse trying to win over the patient, the teacher trying to win over the students, the coach with the players, the business owners with the customers, etc.

To win with people, you must start with **vowing to not be partial**, making the choice to love even the unlovable, forgiving the unforgivable. We must understand that we all deserve respect and love, no matter what we look like or how much we seem to have. I believe one should be treated as if the employee understands the importance that all people are potential customers, and all customers are potential repeated business; after all, they are the lifeline that keeps the business afloat.

Often, we ignore the fact that without customers, there's no business, which also means there's no employees. Consequently, the value of a customer should be very high for employers and employees. So, yes! **Why not stroke the ego?** Let them know you value them, in word as well as in action. Convey to them that without their business, the doors would be closed and bills wouldn't be paid; they deserve to be pampered. That is the key to winning over customers, and turning first-time customers into loyal, die-hard followers. For anyone who wants to be king, you must master the art of winning with people.

Another important factor in winning with people is **to know them and speak their language**. **Understand why they are seeking your service and what it says about them; try to determine their needs and how your business can fulfill it**.

A part of setting up a great, business friendly atmosphere for the customer is them feeling like you are **approachable**, like **they can relate to you**. This is the job of the salesperson as well as the politician: convincing people that you understand their needs, and you have just the solution they've been looking for. Therefore, **effective communication is essential** when dealing with people.

To be able to **control the conversation**, lighten the mood by putting a smile on their face. Also, be sure to effectively communicate the mechanics of what you do, and how you can assist them.

Do not ignore the small things. It is important to acknowledge people and show that you care. Asking people how they are and letting them know you are there to assist them may seem small but they play a major role in winning over a customer, as it makes them feel important.

Counting the Cost to be King

"To avoid criticism, say nothing, do nothing, be nothing." Elbert Hubbard

If you ask most people, I suspect they would tell you that they want to be successful and have the chance to meet their potential; they may even say they would like to die being one of the greatest people to set foot on this planet. In their minds, they flirt with the idea of excellence, perfecting their craft, being number one at what they do, being the most successful employee at their job, being the go-to person in their career. Truth be told, it is only superficial. They would rather be average than to carry the cross, they would rather be liked than be excellent, they would rather have comfort instead of enduring the pain that comes with seeing themselves meeting their potential. In fact, they would prefer to go unnoticed below the radar than take the risk that comes with being number one. Anyone who wants to embark on a journey to reach greatness or self-mastery must make the choice to divorce themselves from being average. Furthermore, to be king, it will take no less, and anyone who wishes to be king must count the cost.

Cost to be King

You will **attract negative as well as positive attention**, you will be **viewed as a threat**, and you **will be hated, criticized, and slandered**. That is the price all great leaders must endure. There's a price tag on greatness, and you can't be afraid to pay it.

In any instance when you decide to part ways with average or the crowd, you immediately **attract attention**. Often, at first, the attention is mostly positive from a select few, perhaps your employer or those who you serve, but eventually it will begin to be drowned out by those who envy your newfound position or success, simply because of their insecurity or the fact that your excellence will begin to expose their average performance. All eyes will suddenly be on you as the praises, recognition, and awards begin to mount up. At that point, the weak will begin to retract, surrender or drawback, folding under the pressure of being under the microscope of those who would rather criticize than to follow or congratulate. However, the strong will do the opposite. They will continue to pounce, stay in the offensive, focus on the service, refuse to compromise their essence, or what they believe to be right. They will welcome the attention as a tool to keep them at their best and to sharpen their skills, and to deepen their newfound habits that are causing them to be successful.

You will begin to be **perceived as a threat**, a light that exposes the average, the incompetent, those who are simply getting by, who simply suck at what they do. This is where the **hate, slander, and chatter** will come from, but also the people who wanted promotions who are proven less qualified than you are, simply because of your newfound success. The truth is that is only half of it, some will hate and slander you, simply to follow the crowd or to be politically correct.

What is important to remember is that often, when you're beginning to be subjected to criticism, it is an indication that you are doing something. You are stepping out of your comfort zone, and slowly breaking away from the pack, and into the major leagues.

You must also remember that those you considered to be great have all paid the same price. They, too, were subject to hostility, hatred, and baseless criticism; however, their greatness eventually drowned out the noise. Examples are many: Jesus Christ, Barack Obama, Martin Luther King, Oprah Winfrey, Michael Jordan, Bill Gates, etc.

Becoming the People's King

What does it take to become the people's king? Well, it takes everything you will learn in this short book. It is a combination of attitude and character, a love for people, and the product you serve them. It is a process of perfecting one's craft. See, becoming the people's king is about increasing in value to not only your employer, but also the customer; it is about understanding submission and allowing it to improve your performance so you can continue to evolve in your space and dominate the competition. It takes an understanding of psychology and the ability to connect to people in ways that they will not forget. However, if I had to summarize it in a few ideas, it would look like this: **mastering your craft, possessing expert knowledge, being perceived as the solution to a problem and as a role model, creating heartfelt impressions, and last, but not least, being hated by the competition but loved by the people.**

Mastering your craft is really about examining your work for the sole purpose of becoming better and better as time progresses. It's about learning how to do what you do more effectively than you've done it in the past; it's about topping your last performance; it's about elevating your value and the service you provide; it's about exceeding expectations on an ongoing basis.

Possessing expert knowledge pertains mostly to your product and business IQ. How much do you know about the product you serve? How much do you understand about the business you're in? Can you help the customer in a manner that is either satisfactory or excellent? Do they look for you when there's a problem with the product or service, are you becoming the go-to guy, the guy who is able to take the initiative to get the job done, the one who is not about passing the buck but, instead, the buck stops with him?

Perceived as the solution to a problem is simply about becoming the guy who the customer would wish every other employee was like. This person is the role model for the company; the one who delivers the service in an excellent manner that should be duplicated or modeled. This person reflects, in essence, what the service should be like all the time.

Creating heartfelt impressions is about being memorable to the point where customers return looking for you. The customer misses you when you're not there because you made them feel valued. Although the service or product might not be perfect, they refuse to go to your competition; instead, they keep coming back for you.

Hated by the competition but loved by the people is about the resistance you will be exposed to when you begin to standout and receive acknowledgement and praise. No doubt the negativity will come. Those who are ignorant of who you are, will hate you. You will shed light on their lack of effectiveness and productivity. It will ignite more jealousy and envy toward you than you can imagine. However, it will be worth it to be KING. After all, all kings were criticized and persecuted, but their impact will always be remembered, for example, Martin Luther KING.

Enjoying the Fruits of Your Labor

"The best revenge is massive success." Frank Sinatra

Why should anyone aspire to be number one, to be crowned Customer Service King? After all, it is not easy. We spoke briefly about counting the cost, and the conscious steps that must be taken to deliver great customer service. Why not just be content with staying under the radar, milking the system for as long as possible, staying clear of the controversy, the criticism, the unfair hostility, the negative attention, and being perceived as a threat. Anyone who has achieved a level of greatness will answer the same: the purpose or the *why* is bigger and much more important than the noise. They went after it because the result would surely outweigh the pain; the dream was worth the hardship. The prize was too great to ignore, doing what's right was better than being dormant, success and meeting their full potential was more rewarding than the sight of failure or the torturing death that comes with being average. They are seekers of success, passion junkies, and the people's champ, company men. They are slaves of greatness and, truthfully, that's what every employer will be seeking in this twenty-first century.

However, what are the benefits of one who mirrors the drive, the mindset, and who has made it to the top of the customer service ladder, otherwise known as Customer Service King? The first is **job security.** While everyone else is anxious about layoffs, that person can rest assured that, one way or another, a spot will be open for them. As long as the business stays open, there is a sense of hope, because they have proven to be of great value to the employer; furthermore, even if they were to be laid off, they have a better chance of coming back, and if they couldn't come back, then they would be able to land a recommendation that could possibly open another door. The benefit is the invincibility that comes with being recognized as one who clearly adds value, and is a great addition to any work force.

Another great benefit to being Customer Service King is being a **candidate for any upcoming promotions**, or raises. Although it doesn't guarantee you will get the opened position, your name will be taken into consideration.

You will also be able to **win influence**, meaning your voice will count. You will be able to influence decisions and get a little bit of what you want. Things you couldn't get away with before, you will certainly be able to now.

You will receive **accolades**, **recognition**, **acknowledgement, and recommendations** that come with being number one.

Last, but not least, apart from a promotion or a raise that can come out of being number one, there is also the possibility of **receiving bonuses, paid incentives, commissions, etc**.

Joseph Vaudy

Life after King

The worse enemy of success is often said to be the last one. After a win, achieving a goal, or overcoming an obstacle, it can be very tempting to become complacent and enjoy your last success more than going head first for the next level. This has been the common denominator or recipe for self-destruction because many who once were at the top found themselves at the bottom shortly after. Life is about striving to become better, enjoying the journey and the successes, as well as learning from the failures to ensure tomorrow is much better than yesterday or today.

It is great to receive the crown, to be at the top of your game, where the prizes are chasing you more than you're chasing them, where everywhere you turn in your company people are thanking, congratulating, applauding, and praising you. However, others may see you as a threat. Often, for every champion comes a day of reckoning or perhaps disappointment, where their focus can't be to maintain where they are, but to dominate the game to the point where they can't be beat. They need to build a work ethic unlike any other, and they need to be as hungry for success as they were before, perhaps even more.

We cannot neglect things that make us prosper. Instead, we must find ways to build on them. If you're at the top, you must continue to lay your bricks and climb higher. If you're somewhere at the bottom, you must do the same and sure enough, you will continue your rise to the top. Never forget that everyone started at the bottom, so you are never hopeless; you should never convince

36

yourself that you can't make it. Keep your eyes on the prize and stretch.

Along the way, we build habits that are either working for us or against us; make sure you create habits that are moving you closer to your desired end, and kill the bad ones. A perfect way of doing so is by doing it right the first time, and continuing to do it right, and eventually it will become second nature. See what works and multiply it by ten, or at least to the level you can.

Life after king can be bittersweet. When you are at the top, everyone can see you. The same thing that helped you climb to the top—consistency, perseverance, passion to be better, and a hunger to serve—can keep you at the top.

Customer Service Made Simple

(50 tips to Customer Service King)

1. Never argue with a customer. Be the peacemaker and the problem solver.
2. Always have a *why* for every time you tell a customer *no*.
3. Do not complain to, or with, the customer; don't stab the company in the back.
4. Become comfortable saying hello to every customer. It puts them at ease.
5. If you don't have the answers, get in the habit of trying to find them.
6. The customer doesn't owe you anything; you need them, they don't need you.
7. Stop focusing on the scoreboard or the money. Focus on the service and the money will come.
8. Put your pride to the side, man up, and apologize.
9. A great personality is an asset to your customer service, so let your light shine.
10. If you wouldn't do it in front of the person who can fire you, don't do it at all.
11. The more versatile and well rounded you are, the better you will be able to relate with people.
12. Treat people how you would want to be treated if you were in their shoes.
13. Use who you are and what you know as a way to connect with people.
14. Customer service has a lot to do with understanding people and meeting them where they are.

15. Nothing is beneath a Customer Service King or a servant leader.
16. Whatever you do, do it with all your heart and strength.
17. Live to meet and exceed expectations.
18. It is often not what you say, but how you say it, so smile more often when you talk.
19. Customer service is always about being the good guy and putting smiles on faces, to inspire and motivate customers to return.
20. You can get away with a lot more when you're nice and attentive to people. Basically, people are more forgiving when they like you.
21. When you love your job, it reflects in your performance.
22. People love and admire people who do what they do and who do it well, so take pride in what you do.
23. A great first impression can make someone a loyal customer, but a bad impression can lose you a customer for life.
24. A positive attitude is necessary to provide great customer service.
25. To be great at customer service, you must master psychology, therapy, ministry, and cleaning.
26. If you don't love and appreciate people, customer service is not for you. Love is necessary.
27. If you see your customers as family, without compromising your integrity and the trust of your employer, customer service will be a piece of cake.
28. Great customer service requires kindness, goodness, gentleness, self-control, patience, and, of course, love.
29. The reward of great customer service will always exceed the investment.

30. People will say and do things to you that you will not appreciate, but how you act when it happens will determine if you are a king, or just the average Joe of customer service. When you know who you are, you have nothing to prove and you can afford to give your pride a break.
31. Aim to be the best and strive to perfect your craft.
32. Remember to thank your customers every time and let them know it is a pleasure to serve them.
33. Under-promise and over-deliver; always find ways to top your service.
34. Built rapport and relationships with your customers. Relationships convert first-time customers to loyal customers.
35. Be accountable. The buck stops with you. When you make a mistake, own it and correct it.
36. Be slow to speak and quick to listen to your customer.
37. Welcome the customer's feedback on your service and use it to make yourself better.
38. Your first customers are the people you work with. A great relationship with them can help you deliver the service you wish to provide.
39. Be consistent with your customer service. Once you raise the bar, you will only disappoint by trying to bring it down.
40. Continue to learn more and sharpen your skills. There is always more to learn.
41. In any relationship, whether personal or professional, great communication is essential, so learn to communicate, connect, and sell.
42. Stay visible, available, and ready to help. Accommodate and please the customer.

43. Watch employee-to-employee conversation when around the customer. Often, they can be offensive to others.
44. Respect and value the customer's money and time.
45. Learn your trade, and be an expert at it.
46. Make them remember you; be memorable in a good way.
47. Don't take anyone for granted, customers especially.
48. Understand that in life, it's mostly the small stuff that counts.
49. In customer service, it is forbidden to be partial.
50. Don't just read the list; learn how to apply it. If you apply the tips, a Customer Service King you will be.

Case Studies

Bryan Karen (Winter Park to Deerfield Beach)

Message: **I'd like to send praise for Joseph Vaudy. He is polite and engaging with all the passengers, including myself, but not in a cheesy way. He is authentic.**

Comment: The keywords in this comment are basically the fact that I was "engaging with all the passengers," which shows that I acknowledged everyone, showed no partiality, and was authentic. I allowed my personality to be the light that shined; I connected with people from point of similarities and also in areas of difference, while still doing it respectfully with a sprinkle of charm, and an approachable posture.

The Devitos (Orlando to New York)

Message: **Joseph's personality and hospitality was awesome and made our overnight trip bearable. He should be praised for lifting people's spirits and keeping them well informed when we were delayed due to the train hitting an ATT van.**

Comment: As a leader, it is important to have the ability to control the mood, and create an atmosphere that is welcoming, comfortable, and business friendly. Therefore, my perception and influence is extremely important in how others will perceive and feel, no matter what occurs while on a 20 hour train trip. After being in an accident, where the passengers would obviously be on edge, it is my job to be as cool as a cucumber, using my skills and temperament in a moment of stress to lighten the mood, without dismissing the seriousness of the situation. At the same time, I need to ensure that everyone is completely safe, and can continue to enjoy their trip.

Nancy Thompson (Orlando to Newark)

Message: **I was on the train 98, leaving from Orlando, Florida to Newark Penn Station. You have one person who was very helpful, polite, and full of energy; he goes beyond the call of duty. His name is Joseph Vaudy.**

Comment: When a customer notices the fact you are going above and beyond, you know you are well on your way to king, because it is saying so much more. This says you are obviously standing out, you care, customer service is a priority to you, etc.

Frenchye Bynes Jone (Savannah to Philadelphia)

Message: **There was a passenger on the train who was loud. She was very abusive to her children and had to be escorted off the train; I just wanted to say that Joseph, the coach attendant, did a great job in diffusing the situation.**

Comment: My job in any situation where I'm dealing with a difficult passenger or customer is always to find a way to understand the situation, control it, and diffuse it so other customers will not be overly affected by it. In this case, another passenger or customer recognized that and went out of her way to make sure someone from corporate understood that I did what I was supposed to be doing. This is also a reminder that people are always watching you, so the show doesn't stop; you must maintain your composure and strive to be your best at all times.

Kesona Bolden (Kissimmee to Newark)

Message: **Vaudy went above and beyond his job description. I have never seen anyone work as hard as he did, and how professional he is and how incredible he made the train environment feel. It was absolutely a change for me and I loved the experience with him on the train.**

Comment: This is a great comment. When a customer, or passenger in this case, says they have never met anyone like you before, it sends a clear message to upper management that this person needs to be looked at, duplicated, or cloned.

Heidi Sequeira (Deland to Miami)

Message: **Outstanding attitude. He was attentive to his cars, and took command of the cleanliness and passenger awareness of upcoming stops. He was friendly and made each passenger feel special, well attended, and important. He also maintained the restrooms in good order, and encouraged passengers to do the same. His were the only cars that didn't smell, and on a long trip from Deland to Miami, that is saying something. I have been an executive for a number of years, and this employee exemplifies leadership. Properly mentored, he will make a great manager. I highly recommend him for your managerial training program. I am extraordinarily impressed. Sincerely, Heidi Sequeira**

Joseph Vaudy

Comment: This is incredible. Here is an executive who happened to be a customer of Amtrak, extremely impressed with the service and letting it be known, even going as far as to say that I should be looked at as a contender for a managerial job. The importance of this letter is the fact that it was written by an executive with years of experience.

Rosemary Williams (Cary to Orlando)

Message: **Joseph gave the very best customer service from the time we got on the train to my destination. He let us know what was going on throughout the trip and knew what time to wake us up and make announcements. I enjoy the trip when he is working because I know he gives the very best service and represents Amtrak very well! He stands out and I remember his name.**

Comment: This passenger is saying so many things that are key to providing good service. First, she is saying from beginning to end, the service is excellent, showing consistency and perseverance. She is saying she loves to see me every time she comes back because she knows what to expect—the best—which means a rapport has been built already and her loyalty is deep.

Diane Felton (Cary to Kissimmee)

Message: **Mr. Joseph made a 14-hour long trip so pleasant; I wanted Amtrak to know that this gentleman went above and beyond what is expected from a train attendant. He made each and every passenger on this train feel special, his professionalism and mannerisms were uncanny. He is a great asset to your company. Sincerely, Diane Felton.**

Comment: A promotion often results from customer recommendations, or is based on the reports coming from the type of service one provides. In this case, where customers are applauding my professionalism and mannerisms, and the fact that I am a great asset, makes this short letter a great recommendation letter.

Ed Nicholson (Kissimmee to Philadelphia)

Message: **Joseph was a delight and made the trip much more enjoyable; he kept the passengers informed about the goings-on aboard the train. He asked everyone personally how he could assist with baggage, cups of ice, meals, etc. I think Joseph can be a model employee for the rest of the train crews.**

Comment: What I love about this is the fact Ed believes I should be a role model for the other train crews. It is saying that I'm definitely standing out in a good way, which is what any employee should want.

Victoria Hargrove (Newark to Lakeland)

Message: **This young man is what I call a train attendant. He made sure I was safely on the train, brought my bags to me, and when I told him I didn't like traveling backward, he moved me to a different seat, and when he went by me, he made sure I was alright. He even asked if I needed anything from the snack bar, now he did come by during the trip and told me he may have to put someone next to me, which was ok. He sat a young lady next to me, she moved because she had no problem**

riding backward. Just a most enjoyable train ride from Newark, NJ to Lakeland, Fl. Different from the ride going up.

Comment: Pay attention to the last part of this message: it was different from the ride up, which means I changed her perception. This is a key task for any employee. She spoke of her experience from beginning to end, mentioning all the small things that ended up making a significant difference to her journey.

Rebecca Miller (Tampa to West Palm Beach)

Message**: I want to say that this is the first time I remember since I've traveled on Amtrak (I've been using Amtrak since 1997 to 1998) that I've received such service. First, the excellent service started before we could even get on the train. Joseph asked us all to line up, where we were going, how many people we were traveling with, and then he came to us one by one to assist and give us seat numbers. Once on the train, Joseph made sure all the guests were comfortable by putting some of their bags overhead, or moving oversized luggage to the back of the car. Joseph let us all know about only having one restroom in service in the car we were in and that if, for some reason, it needed to be cleaned, to let him know so he could clean it before we used it. Joseph walked the car with cups of ice in case any of us wanted any, and even offered to do a food run for us from the snack car. Joseph made us aware of the time the dinner car and the snack car would close so we could get what we needed before they both closed. Joseph cleaned the car as the train was still in service; the first time I've** seen that happen from an employee. When in need, Joseph helped guests with their bags at each stop to make sure the process of the guests getting off the train was smooth and fast. Overall, I was very happy to be on the train today and having seen a wonderful soul as Joseph taking care of so many people's needs. I wanted to make sure that Joseph knows I appreciated the service he offered me and all the help he gave to the guests around me. I did get to tell him that he gave great service as I got off the train at the West Palm Beach stop and gave him a hug. But I felt the need for Amtrak to know about this great team member they have working for them. Please know that I never take time out of my day to say when I get good service on the train, but always make time when I get bad service. This time, my service was so great, that I made time as soon as I got home to sit down to write this up in reference to Joseph. Thank you again, Joseph, for all you do to make guests comfortable while traveling aboard Amtrak. Amtrak, make sure to give Joseph a bonus, even if, as a guest, I have to pay more for my ticket. It would be worth it just so Joseph can be shown how much Amtrak appreciates him and the service he gives to guests. **Rebecca Miller.**

Comment: What I loved about Rebecca's letter was the fact it was long and descriptive. She summarizes, in essence, what most of the other letters have been saying, adding the fact that she never takes the time to speak of the service she receives unless it was negative. However, because the service was outstanding, she felt the need to voice her opinion. She even spoke of the fact that she would love for me to receive a bonus, even if it meant her paying more for her ticket. How amazing.

Ms. Swann (Orlando to New York)

Message: **My attendant was fantastic. He was very personable and helpful. I had difficulty walking, so he kept offering to get me anything I needed from the club car, and he was wonderful and had an upbeat attitude. Thank you for hiring these great people, they restored my confidence in your company. I will be riding Amtrak again soon I am sure.**

Comment: I bring your attention to the second part of the comment. To *restore* means to bring something back to its original state. Even though she had lost confidence in the company, I was able to restore her faith through the service I provided her with.

Ms. Heuser (Washington to Deerfield Beach)

Message: **Joseph was very personable, caring, informative, and outstanding in every way.**

Comment: Personable is another word for relatable, and that is essential when dealing with people; as you become memorable, customers will look for you.

Ms. Rawls (Miami to New York)

Message: **Joseph was wonderful. If Amtrak had more employees like him, they would have a thriving business. Very attentive, especially to seniors and those with disabilities, and he has a good personality.**

Joseph Vaudy

Comment: A great personality will always be an asset, as is doing one's job with a spirit of excellence. This letter highlights the importance of these key issues.

Mr. Black (New York to Tampa)

Message: **Joseph is very courteous. He is the best Amtrak employee I have ever met.**

Comment: Whether I'm the best or not, the fact that he believes so guarantees he will be back again and will more than likely look for me.

Be the King You Are!

We have become so accustomed to the saying "knowledge is power" and have long accepted it for what it is, that we neglect the fact it is not knowledge itself that is power. Instead, it is the application of knowledge. Many people today would admit that they know how to achieve their goals and reach their full potential. But often, what stands between them and the life they wish they could live is "application" —taking the knowledge and applying it to their life.

In this very short book, I have listed many timeless principles that could elevate you to the top of any company, in any field, because all businesses are dependent on one thing: customer service. These are timeless principles that elevated me to the top of my field and resulted in my being crowned the Customer Service King for a multibillion-dollar company. I have simplified what it means to reach the top of your game in the customer service arena so anyone, at any level in the game, can use this information to reach the next level. The formula has been explained so you may take advantage of it and apply it to your life.

This book offers the answers you need to take your career to the next level, whether that means getting a promotion, gaining the highest amount of commission, or receiving the most praises and prizes that comes with being crowned Customer Service King. All that is left to do is for you to join me at the top.

PowerPoint Presentation

Joseph Vaudy

Present

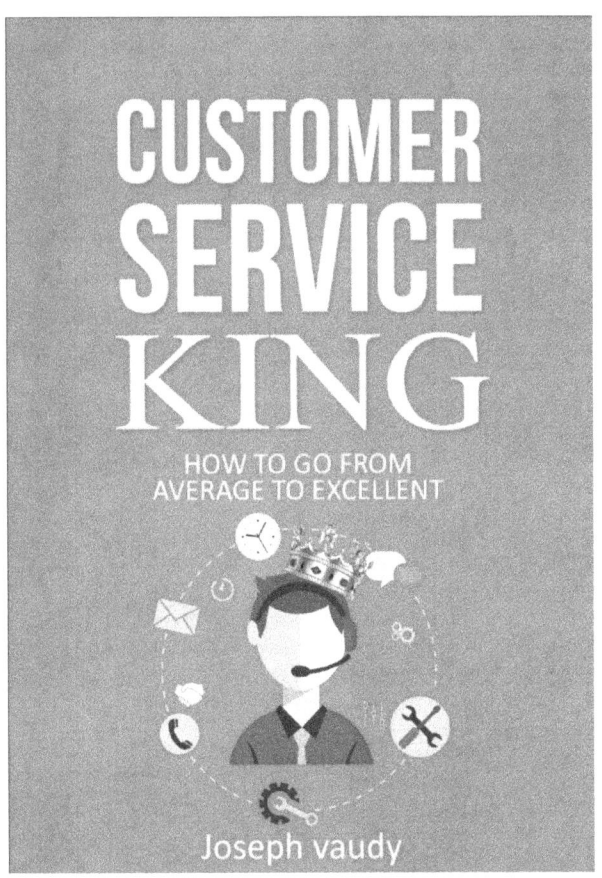

Joseph Vaudy

Customer Service King

How to Go From Average to Excellent

Table of Contents

The purpose of This Presentation!

☐ **First, to ensure you reach Number one or are Crowned Customer Service King,**

☐ **Second, to help you reach a position of influence.**

☐ **Third, to ensure you get what you want.**

How to get to The Top?

☐ Become an Asset to Your Company!

Joseph Vaudy

How did I go From Average to Excellent

The day I became King

Know Thyself!

☐ **Knowing who you are gives you perspective, as it enables you to answer the big questions, such as *Who am I?* This gives you a sense of identity, value, and purpose.**

☐ **When you know who you are within, nothing external can define or touch that, whether it is peer pressure or undeserved insults.**

☐ **When your values and morals are strong, it is easier to not waver or compromise your essence. In other words, you won't sell your soul. You are well able to stand alone for what is right and what you believe in.**

Joseph Vaudy

Understanding the Value Formula

Whatever you don't value properly, you abuse, and whatever you abuse, eventually, you lose.

Understanding submission

☐ **Submission is basically submitting to the will of someone or something else. It is about sacrificing your will or desires to serve someone else's will, which is often advantageous**

☐ **Examples of submissions include:** submission to God, submission to law enforcement or submission to your employer, submission to your parents or your children submitting to you.

☐ **Benefits of submission**: a paycheck, a place to sleep, food on the table, freedom, a trip to heaven, etc.

Mastering Servanthood

- "The Greatest among you will be your Servant."-*Jesus Christ*

- *The path that leads to greatness entails serving the world something it needs.*

- Every business is fighting for one thing: **to serve as many people as possible.**

- **My success as an employee is dependent on how many people I serve, as well as the quality of my customer service skills.**

- **Qualities of a great servant: integrity, humility, motivated by love, passionate, possess expert knowledge, place service before selfishness, and focus on customer service instead of the prize, leaders by heart, and lastly, are able to anticipate needs.**

How to standout

"I want to be different. If everyone is wearing black, I want to be wearing red." – Maria Sharapova

Three keys to the formula of standing out:

☐ Understand what average or the norm is

☐ Understand what is missing

☐ And fill in the blank

Joseph Vaudy

Exceeding Expectations

Four things that will help in regard to exceeding expectations:

☐ **Make going above and beyond a habit**

☐ Don't be content with just meeting expectations

☐ **Take customers beyond satisfaction.**

☐ Last, but not least, give customers a taste of excellence.

Repeat the process over and over again.

Winning with people

- ☐ *"People don't care how much you know until they know how much you care."* - **Theodore Roosevelt**

  How to win with people:

- ☐ **Don't be partial**

- ☐ **Show people you value them**

- ☐ **Know your customers**

- ☐ **Be approachable**

- ☐ **Communicate effectively**

- ☐ **Do not ignore the small things**

Counting the cost to be king

"To avoid criticism, say nothing, do nothing, be nothing."-Elbert Hubbard

- [ ] You will **attract negative, as well as positive attention**
- [ ] You will be **viewed as a threat**
- [ ] You **will be hated, criticized, and slandered.**

Becoming the people's king

A king in the making is:

- ☐ A master of their craft
- ☐ An expert in their field
- ☐ Perceived as a problem solver
- ☐ Perceived as a role model
- ☐ Able to create heartfelt impressions
- ☐ Hated by the competition but loved by the people

Enjoying the fruits of your labor

Benefits of being an asset to your company:

☐ Higher pay

☐ Job security

☐ Promotions/Opportunities

☐ Influence

☐ Accolades, recognition, acknowledgements, praises, and recommendations

☐ Possibility of receiving bonuses, paid incentives, commissions, etc.

Life after king!

The greatest enemy of success is often said to be the last one.

☐ We cannot neglect the things that make us prosper. Instead, we must find ways to build on them.

☐ People see you as a threat and as the person to beat.

☐ Champions dominate the game to the point where they can't be beat. They build a work ethic that is unlike any other, and maintain a hunger for success.

Life after king can be bittersweet because you become a target for all to see, no longer hidden as you climb your way up. But the same thing that had you climbing up, that consistency, that perseverance, that passion to be better, that hunger to serve, can surely keep you at the top.

Customer service made simple (tips)

☐ Always have a *why* every time you tell a customer **no**.

☐ If you don't have the answers, always search for them.

☐ Stop focusing on the scoreboard or the money; focus on the service and the money will come.

☐ A great personality is an asset to your customer service, so let your light shine.

☐ Use who you are and what you know as a way to connect with people.

☐ If you love your job, it will show.

Real Case Studies!

Message: **I'd like to send praise for Joseph Vaudy. He is polite and engaging with all the passengers, including myself, but not in a cheesy way. He is authentic.**

Message: **Joseph's personality and hospitality was awesome and made our overnight trip bearable. He should be praised for lifting our spirits and keeping us well informed when we were delayed due to the train hitting an ATT van.**

Message: **Mr. Joseph made a 14-hour long trip so pleasant. I wanted Amtrak to know that this gentleman went above and beyond what is expected from a Train Attendant. He made each and every passenger on this train feel special; his professionalism and mannerism were uncanny. He is a great asset to your company. Sincerely, Diane Felton.**

Be The King you are!

True or False?
Knowledge is Power

Answer: False
The Application of Knowledge is Power.

**So go be the king you are by applying
the knowledge you
receive.**

the end.

www.ingramcontent.com/pod-product-compliance
Lightning Source LLC
Chambersburg PA
CBHW070931180526
45168CB00003B/1027